T0353164

POCKET IMAGES

Hythe
The Second Selection

Despite the harbour having silted up long ago, ships have been a crucial part of the history of the ancient Cinque Port of Hythe. For centuries it has been in the forefront of our defence against invaders—sending eleven ships against the Armada—and behind this ship can be seen a long line of Martello towers, built to repel Napoleon's forces.

POCKET IMAGES

Hythe

The Second Selection

Joy Melville &
Angela Lewis-Johnson

NONSUCH

An old portrayal of the
east side of the High Street
in Hythe, engraved by J.
Newman. The King's Head
Inn is shown on the left.
Its name has been changed
several times—back in 1583 it
was called The George.
It was in 1750 that its name
was finally changed to the
King's Head.

First published 2002
This new pocket edition 2007
Images unchanged from first edition

Nonsuch Publishing Limited
Cirencester Road, Chalford
Stroud, Gloucestershire, GL6 8PE
www.nonsuch-publishing.com

Nonsuch Publishing is an imprint of NPI Media Group

British Library Cataloguing in Publication Data.
A catalogue record for this book is available from the British Library.

ISBN 978-1-84588-392-8

Typesetting and origination by Nonsuch Publishing Limited
Printed in Great Britain by Oaklands Book Services Limited

Contents

This postcard, showing a cat sitting in a basket chair at an old typewriter with an equally old bakelite telephone by its side, is one of the collective views of Hythe which have remained constantly popular. From bottom left (clockwise) it shows the High Street; the steam engine pulling the diminutive Romney, Hythe and Dymchurch train; the beach; and ducks on the Royal Military Canal.

Another 'good luck' cat, with four slightly different views. From bottom left (clockwise) it shows the canal, with people rowing on it; one of the eighty-eight Martello towers constructed along the coast in 1804; The Ladies' Walk gardens; and 'the smallest public railway in the world'.

Introduction

As there are so many facets to Hythe, we have found it fascinating to compile a 'second selection' of photographs. This time we have created a more literary theme, taking the headings from book titles and using quotations from writers who were involved with Hythe and its environs.

Elizabeth Bowen, the novelist, lived on Church Hill in Hythe and her guests enjoyed the hospitality of the White Hart; H. G. Wells and his family had a residence at Sandgate, the next coastal village to Hythe, as local references in his books testify. H.E. Bates made the Kentish countryside famous in *The Darling Buds of May*.

To balance this, on the scientific side, Sir Francis Pettit-Smith, the inventor of the screw propeller, was born in Hythe and Lionel Lukin, who invented the self-righting lifeboat, is buried there.

It is not only Hythe's famous sons and daughters who deserve praise. The ordinary people who once lived in and around Hythe and helped to make it what it is today are also celebrated. Elizabeth Bowen said of them, 'What comes through so clearly is their strong communal feeling. The Hythe people are bound together by a sense of place; they are both seafarers and farmers. And everyone pulls together. Those who fish are the same men who take out the lifeboats.'

This close-knit feeling extends to the whole town. Families have been settled there for many generations. The unsung sons and daughters have helped forge Hythe's identity—they have made their way up the hill to services at the town's ancient church; staunchly supported the Salvation Army and its band; made colourful and imaginative floats for the town's world-famous biannual Venetian Fête; and been keen supporters of the age-old bowling, golf and cricket clubs.

The same names have been on the shops for decades and as if to repudiate Napoleon's infamous sneer at a 'nation of shop-keepers' the small merchants and artisans of Hythe are still proud to offer service and skills to the fortunate residents.

It is, indeed, to quote Elizabeth Bowen again, 'a nice little town—reassuring and right-and-tight sound. One of the few places that make me love England and Englishness. But I think that apart there's a peculiar quality of Kentishness that I like. The Hythe people are flamboyant and hardy and unmawkish.'

Joy Melville &
Angela Lewis-Johnson
Hythe, Kent

Acknowledgements

Joy Melville and Angela Lewis-Johnson have long been associated with Hythe. Joy lives in both London and Hythe, while Angela, her cousin, lives in Hythe. Both their mothers lived in Hythe. Joy and Angela love Hythe and have particularly enjoyed, while compiling this book, the chance to talk to long-time residents.

Joy has written a number of books, including a biography of Ellen Terry, the actress, who lived at Smallhythe Place in Kent. Angela has collaborated on the illustration and production of various local history books on Kent, Suffolk and Essex. Their first joint book on Hythe appeared in 1995.

We could never have compiled this book without the help and extreme generosity of a number of people who were kind enough to lend their much-prized, historic and loved personal photographs. The authors would particularly like to thank the Hythe Civic Society who allowed them to use photographs including those taken by the late Jack Adams; Peter Wood of Copperhurst, Aldington, and Aldington Parish Council; Kent County Council; Janet Adamson and her colleagues at Folkestone and Hythe Libraries and David and Philippa Hadaway at The Old Gallery Bookshop in Hythe. Others to whom the authors are indebted include John Batten, Jill Blackman, Robin and Ella Blackman and their son Robin, Yvonne Bushell, John and Amanda Champneys, Ian Crunden, Richard Down, M. Eakins, Susan Egerton Jones, Ruth Golding and her son Thomas (www.hythelive.com), Teresa Graham, D. W. M. Hill, Jean Howkins, John Paterson, Sylvia Russ (née Crunden), M. B. Sandford, Richard and Hilda Scarth, Robert Spicer, Jane Sulsh, Charlie Taylor, Monica Thomson, Mike and Janine Umbers and Betty Wood.

We are also indebted to the Civic Society's *The Last Days of Hythe Harbour* by Maurice Young, *Hythe Haven* by Duncan Forbes, Elizabeth Bowen's *Pictures and Conversations* (chapters of an autobiography) and *Elizabeth Bowen*, the biography by Victoria Glendinning.

The friendliness and cooperation of everyone we talked to added immeasurably to the pleasure of compiling this book.

A view of ancient Hythe, showing St Leonard's church, built by the Normans in around 1080 on the site of a stone Saxon church. It also illustrates Hythe's unique character, of being both a coastal and rural town.

One

Down With Skool

This, the first National School in Hythe, was founded in 1814 in the High Street. The school was in a timber-framed Tudor house which was leased from Lady Douglas, with carved figures supporting the gables and upper windows. According to a 1685 plan of Hythe, it used to be called 'Captain Beane's House'. By 1818 the school had 100 pupils. The Church of England had founded the National Society for the Education of the Poor in 1811 and national schools spread rapidly across England. Teaching was by the monitorial system, using the pupils themselves. This system was first set up by Dr Andrew Bell, who had been superintendent of the Madras Military Orphanage.

After years of use by hundreds of children the National School required serious repair. As there was no money for this, the school was relocated in 1844 to an old workhouse in Stade Street while a new school was being built. William Vile, who had become headmaster in 1820, held the position until retiring in 1848. The new school (above) was built in what was then called Hardway's End, but was changed to St Leonard's Road by order of the Commissioners of Pavement. Constructed out of ragstone from the local quarry, it opened as St Leonard's School in 1852, with Edward Palmer as its headmaster. Mass schooling at that time was advocated as a way of preventing pauperism and crime.

The white Edwardian collars of the boys and the starched white pinafores of the girls stand out in this 1903 photograph of the infants school at Saltwood, just up the hill from Hythe. Were they ever allowed to get these dirty? Yet the idea of young children developing their understanding through play was increasingly accepted in the latter half of the nineteenth century. The children in this photograph include Rosie Wire, Tom Godden, Dolly Horton, May Dray, Gwen Smith, Bertha King, Teddie Catt, Albert Smith, Daisy Palmer, Flo Phipps, Ernie Harris, Lily Pitchford, Alice Palmer and pupil-teacher Agnes Rayner. The girls marked with crosses in the fourth row (above) and first row (sitting, opposite page), are aunts of Jill Blackman, who owns both photographs. One of these aunts died recently, in her nineties.

There were various alterations made to St Leonard's School over the years, one of the first being a gothic-type extension (left centre, above). The Union Jack flag, seen here, was flown on occasions like Empire Day. An inspection in 1891 claimed that the boys' school 'maintained its good character' but that the youngest class in the girls' school 'was not very successful in any portion of its work'.

This photograph of the junior school at Saltwood (Standard 3 and 4), was also taken in 1903. At that time, the idea of extending co-education to older children aroused contemporary concerns about the effects of educating boys and girls together after puberty. The children include Reggie Hammon, Annie May, Dick Young, Arthur King, Nellie Johnson, Willie Burton, Mickie West, Tillie White, Hilda Dungey, Norman Loder, Lily Cloke, Mary Johnson, Mabel Catt, Bert Stagg, Lulu Phipps, Johnny Phillips, Ruth Dray, Jim Pitchford, May Morris, Gordon Bowles, Tom Fifield and teacher Mrs Moser.

The Edwardian school-children here are clustered excitedly on the platform at the railway station at Hythe, waiting for the train. School treats by train were comparatively rare occasions and the children can be seen wearing their Sunday best, including large hats and boots. The vicar (bottom, left) is accompanying the party, while the railway porter (right) keeps an eye on the younger participants. Note the platform's decorative overhang and the gas lamp (top, left). There was another railway-owned gas lamp in the road outside and it was the porter's job after

he had locked the station to put out this light, jumping up on a stepping stone in order to reach the chain ring. E. Nesbit, who lived near Hythe, wrote in her book *The Railway Children* of the children's thrill at seeing a train rush out of the tunnel, 'with a shriek and a snort' and then feeling a rush of air as it slid past them, making the pebbles on the line jump and rattle, 'like a great dragon tearing by'.

A CLASS ROOM. MARIST CONVENT. HYTHE.

One of the classrooms in the Marist Convent in Hythe. It is far more austere than classrooms for young children today, which are a great deal more colourful. The main subjects taught in all schools were reading, writing and arithmetic, along with a scripture lesson every morning.

Boys were originally all taught in the one large room (seen above c.1910). The signs saying 'Courage' and 'Truth' were part of the moral atmosphere in which schoolchildren were reared. Children today would barely recognise this as a place in which to learn.

By 1902, there were over 300 pupils at the school. Above is a 1908 photograph of Class 2A in the boys' school. The master standing on the left is Cecil George Molyneux, who was headmaster from 1903 to 1934.

This 1908 photograph of the Standard 6 class in the girls' school shows most of them wearing their best pinafores for the occasion.

Boys from Hythe School, seen here in the early 1950s, planting flowering cherry trees along Military Road to commemorate the opening of Brockhill School for Boys. This photograph came from a former pupil of the school, David Carter of Solway Nurseries, west Hythe.

Boys from Hythe School, seen here in the early 1950s, planting flowering cherry trees along Military Road to commemorate the opening of Brockhill School for Boys. This photograph came from a former pupil of the school, David Carter of Solway Nurseries, west Hythe.

Two

The Old Curiosity Shop

In 1908 the Jacobean Smugglers' Retreat in the High Street was demolished. A number of smugglers operated on the coast around Hythe and a lantern used to be placed in the small tower in the roof as a signal to them. The placard outside the shop below, left, advertises Weldon's Ladies Journal, while that on the right bears the headline 'Tsar Justifies Massacre.'

Four boys in boots and Edwardian collars stand at the beginning of Hythe High Street, a street lined with shops. On the right, under the canopy, shoppers can buy the advertised Lyons tea or stop for refreshments. Outside the shop, the motorcycle carrier forecasts the end of the horse and cart

behind it. The novelist Elizabeth Bowen, who lived in Hythe, wrote 'I like the narrow steep-roofed high street'.

Opposite above: The 'selling' room at Walter & Son's shoe shop in Hythe High Street, *c.*1926. The old ornate, tiled fireplace is still there—even if not draped with shoes any more, but the triangular cushioned seat has disappeared, as this old selling room is now a living room. Customers in those days expected and received courteous and individual attention.

Opposite below: Walter & Son's van portraying 'Russia' in a tableau of Allies organised in 1919 by H. W. Walter to encourage sales of War Bonds.

Right above: Towards the end of her reign, Queen Victoria became less reclusive and more popular, and was heralded as 'Victoria the Good,' and 'The Mother of Her People.' After being Queen for so long, her death shocked the country. Walter & Son's went to town in decorating the upstairs of their shop in a tribute to Queen Victoria when she died in 1901.

Right below: Taking advantage again of the wide space above their shop, Walter & Son's put out the decorations on 'Wakefield Day', during the visit of London's Lord Mayor. The photograph is by Jack Adams, a Hythe resident and prolific professional photographer.

Spicer's high-class grocery shop delighted generations of Hythe people. Harry Spicer came to work at the provisioners called The World's Stores in the High Street in 1918. Shops were struggling then as trading was difficult and rationing was still in force. Bacon was sent unsmoked by rail from London and arrived in a very sticky state. It would be taken up the nearby Stade Street to a small 'herring smoke' where it was smoked with oak dust. It was in Stade Street where the first Spicer's shop (left) was opened in 1926. Although the shop finally closed in 1987, Spicer's moved out to Lympne where it does a roaring trade with its much-sought-after hampers.

You can't miss the eye-catching signs of the J. Sainsbury shop, in the High Street about 1936. The earlier building on this site belonged to Dr Randall Davis, a benefactor of the town, and later became the Wilberforce Temperance Hotel. Next to Sainsbury's is Woolworths, which has occupied the same site since 1934.

Fishmongers, Hythe.

Above: This shop belonged to A. Blackman & Son, the wholesale and retail fish merchants, and used to be in Red Lion Square before it was demolished. The Blackman family have been associated with Hythe for over a century and still have a fish shop in the High Street.

Right: Seen here in the 1920s, in his bowler hat and driving his horse and carriage outside his market gardening shop in the High Street, is Sydney Albert Crunden. With him are his two sons, Steven and Dennis George (in cap). This particular shop later became Boots, but Crunden's greengrocers—now situated in an ancient Kentish Wealdon house—is still a favourite in the High Street. To the left of this photograph is The Green Parrot, which later became Newman's, the furniture shop.

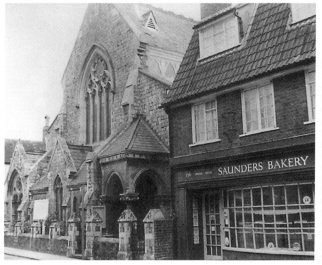

Saunders Bakery, which is now a health and beauty salon, was on the same site for 75 years, although it had to be rebuilt after being damaged by a bomb in 1940. Next to it is the Congregational church, which was built in 1867 and demolished in 1987. It is now the site of new town houses.

Dated 1908, although the view looks remarkably the same today, this photograph shows the ancient town hall in the High Street, with its jutting-out old clock. On the right is the fish shop owned by the Griggs family who, like the Blackman's, have been well known in Hythe for over a century. Traditionally, over the years the Griggs family have not just provided fish, but generation after generation have served as lifeboatmen for Hythe—as well as being staunch Methodists.

Three
Cakes and Ale

An outing of the Ex-Servicemen's Club, with some participants standing and a number of others sitting in the charabanc, centre. Almost all are wearing the standard flat caps, so popular between the two World Wars. The 'Shepherd Neame Fine Ales' sign is prominent on the pub behind them, called The Walnut Tree. This pub was the headquarters of the infamous smugglers known as the Aldington Gang.

Left: The Cinque Ports Arms, at the east end of the High Street, in the late 1940s. Men would spend pleasant evenings in the pub, making half a pint last as long as possible if money was short, talking together and sometimes bursting into irrepressible song as the time wore on.

Below: The children of the Bushell family, generations of whom have lived in Hythe, having a picnic in Edwardian times in front of their little tea-house. Children had to rely on their imaginations to provide home-made entertainment in the days before videos and computer games.

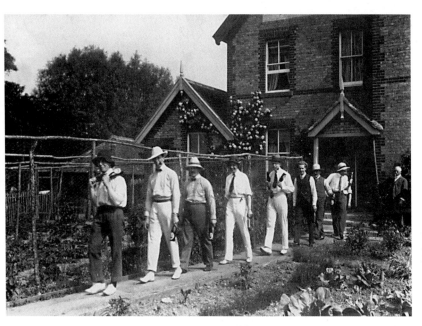

Above: Handwritten on the back of this photograph are the words 'Taking food supplies on board.' Obviously the favoured form of supplies came in small brown bottles.

Right: The Oak Inn in the High Street is now long gone. Next door to the Oak was Tommy Wright's butchers shop, which served Hythe residents for many years. On the left side is the old *bon marché*, with its sign above the shop saying 'Good Value', and its canopy protecting the front.

Above: The Star Inn, in Stade Street, which leads down to the sea, used to have a particularly unusual and distinctive inn sign. It is now a private residence. Like some churches, many pubs have become 'redundant.'

Left: The King's Head has long been a feature of Hythe High Street. One of the first references to it dates from 1583, when it was called The George. It is on the corner of King's Head Lane, which is a small alleyway leading up the hill behind Hythe. This photograph was taken before the Second World War.

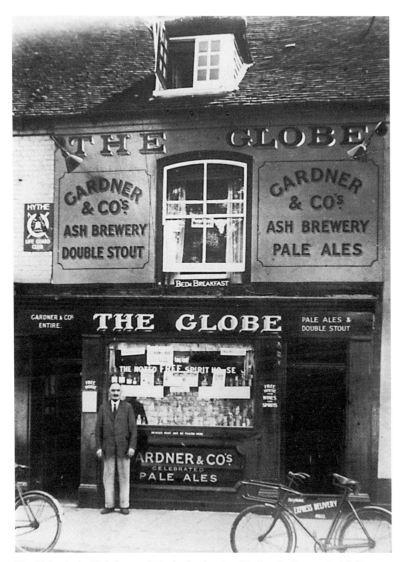

The Globe, in the High Street, which clearly advertises 'Gardner & Company's Ash Brewery Double Stout and Pale Ales', was one of the few pubs not owned by the Mackeson Brewery of Hythe. This photograph, taken in the 1920s, shows the Lifeguard Club emblem up on the left, while in the foreground is a carrier bicycle sporting an 'Express Delivery' sign.

Above: Like the rest of England, Hythe held street parties to celebrate the Coronation of Queen Elizabeth II in 1953. At this one, fancy hats, balloons and smiles were the order of the day. Hythe, as one of the original Cinque Ports, has the right to be represented by a baron at coronations, and at Queen Elizabeth's Coronation it was Sir Frederick Bovenschen, who wore a costume first designed for King Edward VII's Coronation.

Left: Patriotically, the flags and bunting decorate the end of the High Street to celebrate the Coronation of George VI in 1936. The railings were to disappear in wartime. The woman on the left stands in front of a sign proclaiming 'Antiques, decoration, curtains, carpets, productions.'

Above: A family, seen here under a generously decorated building, at the time of the Coronation of Edward VII—a King who was to preside over an extravagant and elegant time of peace and plenty, fondly remembered as 'The Edwardian Era.'

Right: The flags are out down the High Street, enhancing the nostalgic feel of lost days of confidence and sunshine before the First World War. The British flag was ceremoniously saluted on Empire Day, Mayor's Sunday and Armistice Day.

Generations of the Deedes family have been associated with Hythe since the seventeenth century, when John Deedes, captain of the Trained Band of Hythe Volunteers, built the manor house facing St Leonard's church. Between 1640 and 1785, members of the family were mayors

of Hythe no fewer than 22 times. Above, Hythe and Saltwood villagers, including wide-eyed children, are out in force, some pulling the carriage, to celebrate a Deedes' wedding in the early 1900s.

The headquarters of Mackeson's Brewery, at the head of Hythe High Street, when it was decorated for the Victory Parade held in June 1946. The Mackeson sign can be seen over the door on the right, while on the far left an east Kent bus is just appearing in Red Lion Square.

Written on the back of this card, dated 9 May 1913, are the words, 'Do you see me here? Went off very well. [signed] Torie [Victoria]'. The picture it shows of a club's theatricals is addressed to Sapper W. Adams, at 7th Field Company at Chatham, and is lent by Victoria Adams's great grand-daughter Jean Howkins.

Above: An Edwardian fête on the Green at Hythe, held in a marquee. Various flags have been hung under the awning. The servants can be seen standing at the back while the wealthier members of the community sit down in the front, vividly illustrating the 'upstairs, downstairs' character of English society at that time.

Right: A more casual Edwardian family gathering—the Bushell family in this case, having an enjoyable time in a Hythe garden, showing people's capacity for making the most of their leisure time, whatever their level in society. Even today, garden activities are high on the list of favourite hobbies.

Left: The Rose and Crown pub in the High Street, with its ornate plaque, closed in 1971. The advertisement below the plaque reads 'Reliable Shoe Repairs', while the pet shop on the left advertises 'Spillers Shapes For All Dogs'. Next to that is the local grocer, Vye & Son, which used to make daily deliveries.

Below: A church party, in the early 1900s, ready to go on an excursion. Everyone is wearing their Sunday best for the outing. The lengthy open charabanc is large enough to accommodate the whole party, with the folding roof at the back ready for rain. The church, in the countryside near Hythe, is behind the trees.

Four

Fame is the Spur

The drinking fountain used to be next to the town hall, in
the wall of a house belonging to a local doctor, Alderman
Charles Fagge. But in 1912 the London County and
Westminster Bank first demolished and then rebuilt the
house. The year after, 1913, it was placed in Red Lion
Square where it remains. It was recently renovated.

The people of Hythe are proud of the town's banner, seen here alongside an old photograph of the High Street, when the road looked relatively rural.

In 1916, William Cobay, seen above with his official car at the Red Cross Pageant in Hythe, was the mayor of Hythe. The message on the back of this card was sent to servicemen from Hythe during the First World War. It reads: 'I hope you will duly receive the Christmas Pudding which I am sending through *The Daily Telegraph* to every Hythe man serving in His Majesty's Services abroad, about 350 of them. I shall hope to have the pleasure on Xmas Day at dinner of drinking Good Health and Good Luck to all of them, and a speedy, victorious termination of the war.' Each postcard was personally signed by William R. Cobay.

Above: Over the years the town banner virtually fell apart and skilled workers were employed to produce a new one. This photograph, taken in 1981, shows them, alongside the mayor, with the result of their work. Mrs Elsye Melville, the mother of Joy Melville and aunt of Angela Lewis-Johnson, the authors of this book, can be seen third from the left.

Right: A mayor of Hythe, photographed wearing his formal dress and regalia. The list of town mayors, on the wall of the town hall, dates back to the twelfth century in an unbroken line of named mayors, starting with William Hampton in 1349 and continuing through to today. It is believed that Hythe has the best medieval set of records in western Europe.

The Manor House in Hillside Street is one of the few remaining fine large houses in Hythe which were a feature of the 'lower hillside' at the end of the nineteenth century. On a map of 1684, it was labelled 'Captain Deed's House'.

In 1912, Lord Wakefield was driving down to Hythe from the hillside above the town, and was so impressed with the view of the valley leading to the sea that he decided to build a house there (pictured above). He called it 'The Links' and it was a weekend holiday retreat for him and his wife, Lady Wakefield. The local people, according to the *Hythe Reporter*, were impressed by the simple lives the couple led, 'without their cooks, servants, butlers, etc.' During the Second World War, it was used for wounded servicemen and was subsequently bought by Portland Plastics, before being destroyed by fire in 1964.

Above: The Dene, above, on the old Hillside Street (now Dental Street) was formerly the home of the Mackesons, the family who brewed the famous stout, and who were associated with Hythe for 300 years. It was finally demolished and replaced by a terrace of small, pleasant houses, which share the remnants of the former large garden.

Right: This group of houses in Douglas Avenue date from the 1880s. They were named after Douglas of Glenbervi, whose wife came from Hythe.

Port Lympne, the house belonging to Sir Philip Sassoon, who was MP for Hythe during the First World War, and cousin of the poet, Siegfried Sassoon. Prior to that, Sir Philip's father, Sir Edward Sassoon—one of Edward VII's closest friends, had represented Hythe from 1899 to 1912.
After the end of the First World War, Sir Philip built a most attractive residence, Port Lympne, to the west of Lympne Castle. From the outside it looked like an English country house, while inside it was Hispano-Moorish in appearance. It became a key political conference centre, visited by political leaders like Lloyd George and Neville Chamberlain, as well as the Prince of Wales.
In the 1970s, Port Lympne was turned into a wildlife sanctuary and zoo park by John Aspinall.

Oaklands, above, was left to the town by Dr Randall Davis in 1932, with the provision that part of it be used as a museum for the history of Hythe. It is now called the Local History Room. In the 1960s the present library was built in the garden, on the left. The building on the right was originally a stable block.

Five

The Heart of the Matter

Marine Walk Street is one of the narrow side streets leading to the High Street. It lies virtually under the shadow of St Leonard's church. This photograph, taken in the early 1900s, shows the traditional pointed roofs and chimneys of the houses around the High Street and the leisured strolling of passers-by.

The thirteenth-century St Leonard's church, dedicated to the patron saint of prisoners, was both the governmental and social centre of Hythe. It dominated the town and still plays a dual part in the lives of the townspeople, attracting a full congregation on Sundays and carrying out christenings, marriages and funerals, whilst also being a centre of local affairs.

Mount Street is parallel to Marine Walk Street (see previous page). Such streets, many with clapboard exteriors, have retained their character for centuries. This photograph, taken in the early 1900s, shows the beginning of the parking problems that affect even Hythe's quiet streets. In the High Street, at the end of the road, is the National Provincial Bank.

Church Hill, where it joins Bartholomew Street, with Centuries, the old almshouse, on the left. Centuries, with its arched entrance, was built in the twelfth century. The town's almshouse (originally a hospice for lepers and in existence at least as far back as 1336) moved there in 1685. Bartholomew Street may have originally been the waterfront road. In front of Centuries is a large stone, reputedly a bollard to which boats were moored. The flight of steps was not built until 1900 and caused a great deal of controversy because of the difficulty of access with perambulators. Later, railings were added down the middle of the street, to help those climbing up.

Winter-time on Church Hill, looking up towards Castle Road from North Road. The scenery in snow is breathtaking, but the railings are crucial if you are not to slide all the way down. Elizabeth Bowen, who lived on Church Hill, wrote about this part of town: 'Now and then you hear ... distant blowy bugles from Shorncliffe camp.'

Stade Street Bridge, with a distant view of St Leonard's church. This photograph was taken before 1898, when the present Methodist church was built here. The condition of the road is dire, emphasising the need for what is a fine example of a Victorian gas lamp.

A view looking towards Hythe Railway Station taken before 1900 and showing the essentially rural character of Hythe then. St Leonard's church is up on the far right, and there is only one house standing on Tanners Hill. The road that can be seen curving through the centre of the picture is Station Road, with North Road turning away towards the houses and the church. Elizabeth Bowen, looking for a road she first walked along some 60 years before on a previous visit to Hythe, remembered that it had slanted up from Seabrook and zig-zagged across a steep slope, 'finally to merge from a tunnel of greenery and terminate at a high up point where once stood Hythe's railway station'.

A jubilant crowd of Hythe people celebrate the end of the First World War in front of the town hall. On any occasion of importance in the town there are both civic and religious ceremonies, with processions often starting at the town hall and ending at the church. There is a long tradition of holding civic meetings there and the mayor has a special seat in the church. Elizabeth Bowen wrote that 'The town has got the sort of density in its life...that I associate with small towns in France.'

The written message on the back of this postcard is dated 5 July 1905 and reads, 'I am sending you this because I know you have a great liking for weird things'. Pictured is the collection of bones and skulls of some thousands of people stored in the crypt, or ambulatory, of St Leonard's church. There are a number of legends surrounding their origin, but it is now accepted that, at the time of the Black Death in 1349, the number of new deaths required earlier bones in the graveyard to be removed. As there are more bones than can be accounted for by the burial register, some may also have come from flooded churchyards on the nearby marshes.

The photograph above shows the white, wooden Ladies' Bridge over the canal in 1870. The area between that bridge and the next one, Stade Street Bridge, was called 'The Grove'. Lined with trees, it was rural and peaceful.

Stade Street Bridge (also known as the Town Bridge) is seen here before the onset of the Second World War. On the left can still be seen the old tramway lines, while facing it is the Methodist church and its Hall. The bridge was bombed in November 1940 and a temporary wooden-decked Bailey bridge, called 'the Rumbly Bridge' by locals, was erected in its place.

Six

The Lost World

The leisured charm of Hythe's paddling pool and gardens. They used to be situated between Marine Parade and South Road, where the swimming pool now stands. In the background is Lucy's Walk. Some think Lucy is just the name of a girl, as Lucy's Walk runs parallel to Ladies' Walk, both going down towards the sea. Others think it was named after Sir Henry Lucy, the MP, parliamentary writer and *Punch* humorist who died in Hythe in 1924.

Bringing the harvest home in the countryside around Hythe. A traction engine pulls several wagons laden with sheaves of corn or wheat. The smiles on the men's faces reflect the pleasure of getting in the crops, to say nothing of the extra beer and food which usually followed. It was the 'crown' of the year's work.

Here, the sheaves have been made into a stack, which can be seen behind the wagon. The stack was probably thatched to protect it from the weather. The sticking-up poles helped contain the load and later the sheaves would be threshed to separate the ears from the straw. The shape of the farm wagon is practical and attractive. To us, today, it has a strong nostalgic appeal recalling, indeed, a lost world.

Threshing machines on hire would go from farm to farm. These machines, powered by a traction engine (far left) would separate the grain from the straw. The straw would then be used for animal bedding and possibly thatching.

These men are probably thatching the building on the right with the straw—i.e. the stems left from threshing the ears from the corn. The wooden ladder was hand-made from tall saplings.

Left: We may have lost much in recent years but the relationship between 'one man and his dog', symbolised here by the gentle, reassuring touch on the dog's head is still alive and well in the countryside.

Below: A farm labourer using wood for making hurdles, fencing, gates and stakes. Wood has always been crucial for day-to-day farming needs. Chestnut trees are still managed and 'coppiced', in order to produce sufficient wood for requirements. This practice ensures good management of woodland and has been carried on since the Middle Ages.

Despite the smile, a great deal of strength and skill are needed to shear a sheep. Out on Romney Marsh, shepherds were called 'Lookers'.

The farm machines of the early 1900s look incredibly antiquated to our eyes a century later. Here, the sheep shearers proudly line up with sheep that have been denuded of their fleeces. Wool was a valuable commodity and brought riches to England in past ages.

Above: Clothes make a social comment. The patriarch standing by the side of his sitting wife exudes respectability. Many clergy did what they could to help their parishioners and were often treated with a mixture of respect and restraint, owing to the difference in status.

Left: Mary Christmas, wife of the ploughman, was also an artist's model. Here, in costume as a peg seller, she may look a picturesque figure to our eyes, but in reality the life of a working farmer's wife in those days was hard—though it could also be very rewarding.

Above: The local worthies seen here would take it as their natural right to run local affairs. No woman is in sight, nor in the early days of the twentieth century would they expect to be consulted.

Right: Contrast the fashionable hat, breeches, white cuffs and neat handkerchief with the clothes worn by the labourers on the previous page.

Seen here, around 1903, standing outside their thatched farmhouse, is the Franks family. The dog and horse are very much part of the family, as indeed is the lamb!

56

This picturesque timber building with its distinctive tall chimneys is something of a mystery. No information has come forward as to its purpose, unless, as the clothing on the washing line suggests, it was simply a dwelling place.

The days of the blacksmith in his smithy were ending and ironmongery was taking over. Blacksmiths extended their skills to make gates, railings, tools and household items. Here, A. N. Banyard stands in front of his shop, with horse collars still on view on the left. On the right is a bicycle, which was becoming a preferred form of transport, and smiths tried their hand at mending both bicycles and cars.

Right: A windmill of the type that was common in and around Hythe. The device on the right catches the breeze and turns the sails to the wind. Although there were some half a dozen working mills in the town, the only remaining one now is a watermill at the east end of the town, and which is still inhabited.

Below: The quarries at Aldington, near Hythe, looking towards the Walnut Tree Inn, which was the headquarters of the famous smugglers the Ransley gang, whose leader was hanged at Maidstone. There was another large quarry—of Kentish ragstone, on the northern slopes of Hythe, below Saltwood Castle. The slopes were known as Quarry Hill.

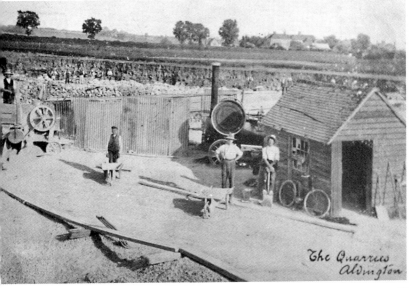

The Quarries Aldington

Potato-picking in the 1920s. Kent has long been known as the Garden of England and excellent fruit and vegetables are still produced here. Signs on fields today invite passers-by to pick their own strawberries and other fruits. Workers in the Kent fields in earlier days had to work long hours on subsistence pay but found the work satisfying, as well as enjoying the rewards of fresh produce.

Opposite above: Ploughman Charlie Christmas, whose wife Mary can be seen on page 54—is pictured here at work with two farm horses. His life was as tough as his wife's—up and out, usually before daybreak, after a breakfast of bread and lard, and taking with him a dinner-basket prepared overnight by his wife.

Opposite below: Land girls in the countryside around Hythe during the Second World War. From left to right: Nancy Brooks, Edith Stone, Mrs Head and Mrs Appleton. They were invaluable to farmers who had lost most of their labour to conscription.

Left: Childhood in Hythe in the early twentieth century certainly *looks* idyllic. This photograph shows two youngsters belonging to the Bushell family in front of their summerhouse, enjoying the timeless games of children.

Below: A leisurely row down the Hythe Canal by members of the Champneys family of Otterpool Manor. Women used to be regarded as ornamental, so could sit back, shaded by large hats, and not be expected to help with the rowing.

7 HYTHE. — The Grove. — LL.

Above: The scene in the Grove in 1911. This attractive area of grass and trees lay between two of the Royal Military Canal's bridges. Hats were the accepted wear and the pace of life was leisurely, causing us to look back on it nostalgically as a lost 'Golden Age'.

Right: Note the penny-farthing look of the large Edwardian baby carriage, echoed in the smaller dolls' carriage which is being pushed by one of the Bushell children along the garden path, with its carefully marked-out edges. Gardening is a passion among many residents of Hythe.

Cutting the edges of the grass in the 'American Gardens', in the grounds of the Garden House, Saltwood, overlooking Hythe. Working in large gardens was hard, and it could take years to work up from an under-gardener to a head one, but the job did at least offer security and an outdoor life.

Opposite above: Mrs Champneys in Edwardian times standing in front of Otterpool Manor, in the countryside near to Hythe, where the Champneys family have lived since the seventeenth century. On one outside stone wall are the carved initials 'RC' (Richard Champneys) with the date '1633'.

Opposite below: The formal capes and hats that the Bushell family children wore, like all children reared in Edwardian times, must startle contemporary children into wondering how they managed to play in any relaxed way. E. Nesbit's stories, including *Five Children and It*, give an insight into the flavour of life at that time.

A local fair before the First World War, with the merry-go-round looking just the same as it does today. The fire engine in the foreground used to belong to Bilsington, near to Hythe, but it was eventually to end up further away in Kent, at Lydd.

Seven

War and Peace

The Grove, alongside the Royal Military Canal. Since its construction began in 1803, the canal has been part of the county's military defences. But for well over a century afterwards it was regarded as a delightful asset, used by local residents for rowing along, or walking beside. The people shown sitting there peacefully before the First World War had little idea that the very area where they were sitting would be cleared only a comparatively few years later, in order to erect a war memorial.

Officers in No. 5 Squadron at the School of Musketry in 1890. The vast wheels of the gun carriage practically hide the gun. Moustaches were in vogue for military men in those days. To be 'Hythe trained,' according to a former Lord Lieutenant, was a mark of excellence.

Canadian Army captains, with moustaches again in evidence, congregate on board a boat at Hythe. All are wearing rather cumbersome life jackets, still necessary today for a trip on the changeable English Channel.

Soldiers standing outside the School of Musketry in Hythe before the First World War. The school was established in 1853 and Hythe became a military town. A number of fine buildings were constructed to house the men, and generations of soldiers came to know Hythe and add to its prosperity. This photograph includes two visitors from the Antipodes.

Army students were quartered in the two white buildings (right) which were named Hay and Halliday after the first two commandants of the Hythe School of Musketry. The Officers' Mess was housed in the ivy-covered building in the foreground. To the left of the Mess was Travers Library, named after Colonel Travers, another of the early commandants. He bequeathed many of the books which formed the archives of the school.

The Royal Military Canal before the beginning of the First World War. The boat station on the left looked west towards Stade Street Bridge. Boating on the canal had been a popular pastime for many decades. Those watching above are sitting on terraces, while the boat in the centre seems to be attracting attention, particularly from the boy scout on the left. The novelist Elizabeth Bowen remembered that as a child, 'Our Military Canal was not the less seductive for boating-picnics,' but when it was dug, between 1805–1809, its purpose

was solely military. This was because in 1804 there was a great scare that Napoleon was on the verge of invading Britain. The defence plan was to construct a canal which would cut off the Dungeness Peninsula from the rest of England, acting as both defensive ditch and communications channel. It was the idea of Lieutenant Colonel John Brown, and was 28 miles long, 60 ft wide. Gun emplacements were positioned every quarter of a mile along.

A Canadian ambulance, driven by a major, in Otterpool camp during the First World War.
A number of soldiers from the Canadian Expeditionary Force were billeted at the camp which
was only a short distance from Otterpool Manor, near Lympne. Many Canadians were killed
at Ypres and some of the wounded came to convalesce at Shorncliffe Camp on the cliffs above
Hythe (including Roy Melville, the father of Joy Melville and uncle of Angela Lewis-Johnson, the
compilers of this book) and at Otterpool Camp. Ironically, they were then at risk from the first
lot of bombs dropped by German Zeppelins. One of these caused casualties in the camp and
made the horses stampede, though the town of Hythe itself escaped.

This shows the Metropole Laundry van being used as a makeshift ambulance. This was a
practice run at the beginning of the Second World War. The Pavilion has a sandbagged
entrance, ready for action and the van has been stripped of its normal shelves. The Metropole
Laundry's dry cleaning was a speciality and it also beat and cleaned carpets.

Right: Kathleen, a First World War Red Cross nurse, was one of the Champneys family from Otterpool Manor. Many girls received their first taste of freedom in such wartime occupations.

Below: The Boys' Camp on Hythe Green. Soldiers frequently camped on the Green and one elderly resident of Hythe recalls that he and other boys used to be asked by soldiers who were not allowed to leave the Green if they would go and get them a fish and chip supper for 3d. Soldiers would often camp for some three months in the summer, coming down from Shorncliffe camp in order to practise firing on the Hythe ranges. They would march into Red Lion Square, with an accompanying Army band playing.

Armed soldiers are an unexpected sight in Bilsington, a peaceful village near Hythe. But the dearth of traffic and yellow lines is a reminder of what villages used to be like. As Laurie Lee was to observe, villages used to have a sense of place, and not just be a passing point on the way to somewhere else.

Otterpool Camp, at Sellindge near Hythe. On the right, in the background, is Otterpool Manor. The words on the top of this postcard are '5th Amb', short for 5th Field Ambulance. The message on the back of the card, addressed to 'Lieut. Selater,' originally read 'Is Capt Wright with you now as I have sent him a pc [postcard] addressed to 6th Field Amb.' This has been scored out and the anodyne words 'It has been a nice day today,' have been substituted, suggesting possible censorship.

Otterpool Manor where the Champneys family have lived since the seventeenth century. A certain Thomas More carved his initials over the barn ('TM, 1729') while staying at the Manor when he was designing the Hythe Military Canal. The present owners, John and Amanda Champneys, now run the 370 acres as a farm. 'My father used to have a sheep farm,' says John, 'but in those days there were three families living here. Today it's hard for just one family. We've had to cut back and we now have all the land as arable, as wheat.' There is still a friendly family atmosphere, though, with logs and eggs for sale along with occasional fruit and vegetables.

Canadian troops were stationed at the Manor during the First World War and officers used the home as their base. These soldiers are being served tea (perhaps their first unexpected introduction to the English custom) in the front garden of the Manor by members of the Champneys family. The first public bus to operate started in the First World War. Its route was from Folkestone to Otterpool Camp and back, and it was organised to take the troops to town.

Left: Dr W. S. Tucker in front of the new 20 ft sound mirror (an early radar dish) on the Roughs at Hythe in 1923. This mirror survived until the 1980s, when it collapsed due to land slippage. As Director of the Air Defence Experimental Establishment, Dr Tucker was the scientist in charge of research into acoustic defence systems between the World Wars.

Below: A 30 ft sound mirror, built in 1929 on the Roughs at Hythe. The photo was taken by Richard Scarth, the Hythe author of *Mirrors By The Sea* and *Echoes From The Sky*, which tell the story of these unusual structures.

Opposite above: A collection of our wartime defence measures: the rear view of the 1929 30 ft sound mirror, with the Martello towers and firing ranges in the background.

Opposite below: The great size of the Hythe sound mirror—an extraordinary sight to come across in the apparently tranquil countryside, can be seen here in comparison to a human figure. What can also be seen is the appalling amount of graffiti and damage by vandals which, sadly, has seriously increased recently.

Firefighters look up at the devastation in Hythe's High Street during the Second World War. Hythe, being so near to France, was shelled from coastal batteries located on the cliffs at Cape Gris and was also the target of high explosive and flying bombs. A great deal of property was destroyed and the war memorial records 60 deaths. Many more were injured. Hythe prepared itself as well as possible for the war. In the Spicer family's history, 'Spicer's Seventy Years', it is recalled that after the end of the phoney war, 'The Stade Street bridge over the Canal was

blocked with a large steam roller, sandbags on either side. Ladies' Walk Bridge was demolished—as were, in fact, all footbridges, leaving just the four road bridges. Mass voluntary evacuation was requested. Many responded immediately, leaving the breakfast table with the dirty cups and plates and food still there, and not even bothering to turn off the light, gas or water. The schools were transferred completely to South Wales but ... there remained nearly three thousand people in the Town.'

Hythe is used to colourful military marches. W. S. Miller in his book, *The School of Musketry in Hythe,* comments that the 'Life Guards, Blues, Dragoons, Lancers, Hussars, Guardsmen, Highlanders, Riflemen, Fusiliers, Royal Marines, Militiamen and Volunteers, with a sprinkling from the West India Regiments and Lagos Constabulary, combine to form a picture which, for variety of uniform and brilliance of colouring, is quite unique'. Above, watched by the townspeople, the Small Arms Wing of the School of Musketry marches out from Hythe in 1968, past the Grove Cinema and the summer theatre—which was based in the Hythe Institute. Both the cinema and the Institute were later to be demolished in the interests of road-widening.

Eight

On the Beach

The old Hythe lifeboat. Before the days of the motorized lifeboat the crew had to use sail and oars. The lifeboat is greatly missed as the English Channel is one of the busiest shipping lanes in the world and therefore extremely hazardous.

It was Colonel Twiss, Commander before Sir John Moore, who recommended the building of massive, round Martello towers, which would act as sea batteries to fight off the threat from Napoleon. Twenty-seven towers alone were built on the Kent coast between 1805 and 1808. They were about 30 ft high, three-storied, with brick walls and a platform at the top which supported a twenty-four pounder gun. There was accommodation for one officer and twenty-eight men, who climbed up by ladder on the landward side. Ammunition was stored at ground level. Above, two men stand on the ruins of one of these towers. Some that were still standing were brought back into use in the Second World War. Twiss Road in Hythe commemorates the Colonel.

A ride on a donkey on the beach was for years an expected part of any child's holiday by the sea. Donkeys were always a high spot, along with the Punch and Judy man, and indeed any seaside town unable to produce either of these would fall down the popularity scale. Hythe was high on this scale for many years.

High seas in front of Hythe's Imperial Hotel. The sight of the sea crashing over the promenade has long been one of the local excitements but since the sea defence work of 1996, scenes like this are no longer such a danger. People living on the seafront, or in nearby streets, are thankful for this, but the sea is still spectacular when it is rough, and remains a dramatic feature of life on the coast.

Paddling in the sea when it was calm was a very different experience from the rough seas above. This photograph also depicts the tranquil life that existed before the onset of the First World War. People still travel many miles to the coast and they, as well as locals, enjoy walks on the promenade, often going as far along as Sandgate when the weather is favourable.

51013.

Relaxing on the seafront at Hythe in 1922. The line of Martello towers can be clearly seen here. Elizabeth Bowen, who lived in Hythe, wrote about it in her novel, *The House in Paris*, saying, 'Centuries ago the sea began to draw away from the cinque port, leaving it high and dry with a stretch of sea-flattened land between town and beach. The grey barracky houses along the sea are isolated; if the sea went for them they would be cut off.'

Opposite above: The Parade, Hythe, before the First World War. Large-wheeled bathing machines are lined up in front of the sea, so that hardly anything could be seen of the decently-clothed ladies, leaving them to swim. The two young ladies strolling along on the left are wearing fashionable tight belts, soft ties and straw hats. Fishermen have boats moored on the beach and are drying out their fishing nets. The beach at Hythe, once sandy, has long been covered up by shingle.

Opposite below: On the back of this postcard is wriiten, 'Jack is better able to be carried downstairs and out in a Bathchair. The hurt is a little above the ankle.' The date is 1904 when bathchairs were a common sight on the seafront.

These balconied houses on the seafront were known as Saltwood Gardens and it is said that they were built for officers and their families who were serving in the town. There is a wide variety of architecture in the town, including Kentish ragstone constructions, clapboard-faced cottages and timber-framed buildings as well as modern brick houses. Each era has made its own contribution.

Bathing huts and deckchairs were the order of the day in the 1920s. The large building at the back was Moyle Tower, which brought a number of visitors into the town when it was used as a Christian holiday centre in the 1920s and 1930s.

The luxury Imperial Hotel, Hythe's grandest building, was originally a railway hotel called the Seabrook, which was opened in 1880. It was renamed in 1901, celebrating the heady days of Victorian splendour. Inside, the silk tapestries on the couches and Axminster carpets attracted many guests, while in the large grounds outside were tennis courts and croquet lawns. The tramlines in front of the hotel brought guests right to the door. They are long gone now, and the terraces have also been filled in. But today the hotel remains very popular, with many guests making use of its attractive golf course, which runs alongside the sea.

The Pavilion at Hythe, situated on Marine Parade and the corner of Stade Street. The two people sitting restfully outside it confirm it as a place for leisure activities. The swimming pool is now nearby. This photograph offers a contrast with the wartime picture on page 73.

The Parade, Hythe seafront, in 1918. Many of the houses had shutters to keep out the sun, and deckchairs had small canopies above them, as it was still unacceptable for ladies to be sun-tanned. Small children in those days wore hats almost as large as the ones worn by their

mothers. Perambulators were far larger than they are today, as there was sufficient space to push them with ease. Today, skateboarders, joggers and bicyclists make walking anywhere more hazardous.

Above: Fishing boats moored up on the beach at Hythe. The fishermen returned about three or four o'clock in the morning. Today, the Griggs family, part of the fishing community for nearly a century, run The Fish Shed, only a few yards from the beach, which sells a variety of different fish and is well patronized.

Left: Hauling a fishing boat down to the sea, in the Edwardian era, on the same stretch of beach. These boats are the traditional kind along this coast and fishermen and helpers haul them up from the beach with winches. In earlier times the great Cinque Port Fleet used to sail from here to Great Yarmouth each autumn, on its way to the Herring Fair at Great Yarmouth.

Hythe's old lifeboat under sail, at sea, manned by a full crew. Over the years, the seafaring Griggs family have usually had at least two of its members acting as part of the lifeboat crew.

Wright Griggs, with his patriarchal white beard, seen here with his eldest son John, carrying out the laborious but necessary task of mending fishing nets.

The Hythe Lifeboat being launched. Both the boathouse and the lifeboat were presented by Viscount Wakefield of Hythe in 1936.

A photograph of the Life Saving Rocket Company, Lade Station, No. 2 Battery, Dungeness, taken in 1915.

Nine

This Sporting Life

A shooting party in the 1950s at Bilsington, near Hythe. Shooting is a deep-rooted country tradition, with participants enjoying the sport and the company, as well as the scenery and the food, all of which were part of a good day out.

94

The Hythe Golf Club House in the early years of the twentieth century, with members standing at the door. Golf clubs are stacked in the back of the car, under the hood, and the lacy balconies seen not only here but in other Hythe buildings, were commented on by Elizabeth Bowen. She said of Hythe, 'I found myself in a paradise of white balconies, ornate porches, verandahs festooned with roses, bow windows ... fantasy buildings, pavilions of love.' Shortly after the onset of the Second World War the Golf Club was closed down, and was ultimately replaced by the Sene Valley Golf Club.

Opposite above: The cricket pavilion in Hythe, which stands on the south bank of the Royal Military Canal. The earliest recorded match of the prestigious Hythe Cricket Club was against the School of Musketry in 1855. During the Second World War, a German bomb wrecked the pitch, which must have caused more pain to some than the majority of bomb-damage!

Opposite below: A local game of boys' cricket in Hythe. Rather surprisingly, the two batting are women—they were quite possibly teachers. In those days women cricketers often had to wear lead at the bottom of their skirts, to prevent any scandalous possibility of them flying upwards.

It's surprising that bowls ever survived in England, given the fact that William IV banned it, because it diverted young men from taking part in archery practice, and that in 1477, Edward IV passed a law ordaining 'that anyone found playing bowls was to be imprisoned and fined £10'. The exact date that Hythe's Bowling Club started is not known, except that it was founded before 1652. The 1907 flat-roofed pavilion was renovated in 1939 and given a pitched roof and a new front face with two small, decorated gables (see above).

Opposite above: Anyone for Tennis? A Victorian tennis party where the wooden racquets are elongated and shaped more in the style of lacrosse sticks. Compare these long dresses with the far less cumbersome attire worn today. The matriarch, with shawl and cap, looks on.

Opposite below: The player in the centre holds a football which reads, 'Hythe Football Club, 1949–50'. This was the Kent Amateur Junior Cup, which Hythe reached the final of in two successive years. They were runners-up the first year and won the second year.

Two riders from the Champneys family in front of their home, Otterpool Manor. Riding is a perfect way of seeing the countryside around Hythe, as you get a chance to see over the many hedges.

Rowing on the Hythe canal is often less leisurely and more exhausting than the visitor might expect. Here, the boats are lined up on the bank by the boathouse, which sports a patriotic flag.

Ten

I Capture the Castle

The romantic ruins of Saltwood Castle, overlooking Hythe. This particular part is the entrance and north tower. The fourteenth-century gatehouse is the main residential part.

Lympne Castle, before its restoration in 1905 by its new owner, and the adjoining church of St Stephen, which dates back to the twelfth century. Lympne was an important port in Roman times, before the coastline changed, and below the castle you can see the broken masonry, which is all that remains of the Roman fort, *Lemanis*.

A solitary visitor sits in front of Lympne Castle. In Norman times the Archbishop of Canterbury owned the land and a fortified residence was built. This ultimately came into private hands and by 1905 had dwindled into a farmhouse. This remained the case for some years but more recently the Great Hall has been used for functions and festive occasions, with dancing on the terrace overlooking the marsh on dusky summer evenings.

Saltwood Castle at its most imposing. The castle was once the home of the Archbishops of Canterbury but was almost entirely rebuilt around 1160. It was turned into a dwelling in 1885 and some repairs were authorized by Sir William Deedes when he was living there at the end of the nineteenth century. It then fell into a ruinous state and little was done until a new owner in the 1930s had a new residential wing constructed and the gatehouse restored. The castle was ultimately bought by the Clark family and the late Alan Clark MP died there.

The castle has always been a major attraction to visitors. Here, some can be seen exploring the ruins. The castle is now a private residence, no longer open to the public. One of the fascinations about the castle is that reputedly the four knights who killed Thomas a Becket stayed there the night before, rode to Canterbury to kill him and then galloped back at speed to the Hythe coast, before embarking for France.

The front view of Sandgate Castle, which was built by King Henry VIII. It is on record that 100 tons of stone and eighty tons of oak were taken from nearby Monks Horton Priory, which Henry had ordered to be destroyed. More stones were probably taken from nearby St Radigund's Abbey, also destroyed. The castle was visited by his daughter, Elizabeth I, in 1573 on one of her frequent peregrinations that often almost bankrupted her hosts.

Westenhanger is on the Roman road that leads from Hythe to Canterbury. The castle was a Saxon palace originally built by the kings of Kent, rebuilt by the Normans and turned into a fortified house in the fourteenth century, when it was given no fewer than nine towers. The Tudors topped this by adding 126 doors and 365 windows. Today, a fragment of the fourteenth-century wall remains, along with three towers and a Tudor doorway. One of these towers, the Round Tower, was for centuries a dovecote for 500 birds.

Eleven

The Old Brigade

The Hythe fire brigade, lined up in front of the old fire station, which was built in 1925.
This building is now the Hythe Garage and the date can still be seen on the façade.

The Hythe fire brigade in their helmets, along with their fire engine, taken in the year 1905. An interested crowd looks on, including, on the extreme left in the bowler hat, Mr William Cobay, the popular mayor of Hythe.

In 1906, the Hythe fire brigade got a new steam fire engine, the Speedwell. Here it is being conveyed down Hythe High Street, with small boys excitedly running alongside the trotting horses while the firemen stand tall. Griggs, the fishmonger's, is on the right, and Bushell's gentlemen's outfitters is on the left.

Six members of the fire brigade at Bilsington, a village near Hythe. Professional though they look, they might have encountered problems if called on to go any distance with what looks like a rickety cart.

The Hythe fire brigade was a much larger contingent than that of Bilsington. Four sit neatly cross-legged while the rest, all helmeted, stand in front of the extending ladder on the engine. One young would-be member is enjoying the experience of being next to the driver.

In 1907 there was a fire at the 'Sportsman's Inn', owned by Mackeson's Brewery, in the High Street. Smoke is partially blocking out the names of the buildings, while an interested audience looks pretty unconcerned. Later a cinema was built on this site and later still the Arcade was erected there. This in turn was bombed in 1940 and destroyed.

The mid-sixties' scene of the fire at Newman's, the furniture store. Carpets that have been saved are stacked on the High Street. There was a second fire in 1984, but after both events the shop was rebuilt to look just the same. Newman's served Hythe for many years but has now closed.

Hythe firemen standing in front of a rather more elegant vehicle than on previous pages, with the ladder fixed on to the roof and the hose on-tow behind.

Twelve

The Loved One

A gathering of the Champneys family in front of the family home, Otterpool Manor, near Hythe, in the early 1900s. At the time there were fourteen family members living there, including six children.

The store above, with the overhead signs that read 'Hosier. Tailor. Outfitter. Wm. Bushell. Boot Warehouseman' belonged to the Bushell family, well known in Hythe for many years. Another small sign says 'Propeller House' and this, together with a further plaque above, commemorates Sir Francis Pettit-Smith, who was born in this house in 1808, the son of a Hythe postmaster. Sir Francis (nicknamed 'Screw' Smith) was the inventor of the screw propeller for steamships, which proved far more effective than the paddle-wheels which had been in use until then. Ships could now be run at greater speeds and at a cheaper rate. The first ship to use the screw propeller was the S.S. *Archimedes* in 1839, and was so successful that within the next ten years a further 100 ships had been built equipped with screw propellers.

The gravestone of Lionel Lukin, in St Leonard's church, Hythe. Lukin, who was born in Essex but came to live in Hythe, invented the buoyant 'self-righting' boat. This inscription reads: 'This Lionel Lukin was the first who built a Life Boat and was the original inventor of that Principle of Safety by which many lives and much property have been preserved from shipwreck and he obtained for it the King's Patent in 1785.' On the front of the gravestone it reads: 'In this grave is interred the body of Lionel Lukin'.

Above: The seafaring Griggs family, who feature in the section 'On the Beach,' seen here in the year 1906. The Griggs family came to Hythe bringing coal for the gasometers by boat from the north, and became the mainstays of the local fishing fleet.

Right: Another family which, like the Griggs family, has long been involved in the fishing industry is the Blackman family. Here, Mr and Mrs Robin Blackman, with Robin Junior, the father of the present Robin Blackman, who is the fishmonger in Hythe High Street.

Above: The esplanade at Sandgate (the next village along the coast from Hythe), towards Dover, was where the writer H. G. Wells chose to live. After his health broke down in 1898, he bought a piece of property at Sandgate and commissioned the architect C. F. A. Voysey, famous for his late Victorian houses, to build one for him. Called Spade House, it had a great sea view, thick walls, a garden and croquet lawn. H. G. Wells and his family were to live there for nearly a decade.

Left: Church Hill, Hythe, after the Second World War, in a rather more dilapidated state than now. Elizabeth Bowen lived on the hill, having bought a newly-built house there because Hythe was full of the memories of her mother who had once lived in the area. She was to write: 'On its inland side, the town climbs a steep hill, so that the houses stand on each other's heads. The beautiful church must have crowned the town; now new houses spread in a fan above it, driving back the thickety hazel woods. Back from the brow of Hythe hill the country – cornfieldy open and creased with woody valleys, Kentish, mysterious – stretches to the chalk downs.'

Thirteen

The Music of Time

The Salvation Army band marches along Hythe High Street, past the pork butcher's. A couple of interested Edwardian boys walk alongside. Today the Hythe Salvation Army band is in great demand locally. In the summer it performs regularly every Sunday, marching up Stade Street, and playing on the seafront and in Red Lion Square. In the winter it plays at indoor meetings at the 'Citadel'.

William Booth founded the Salvation Army in 1878 and recruitment spread rapidly. They became well known through their custom of playing music in the streets, believing this an important way of attracting people's attention and passing on their message. Here are five of the daughters of the Griggs family of Hythe, who were all members.

Four ladies in the senior Salvation Army band in the 1950s. From left to right: two cousins, Ena Mills (trombone) and Mary Jones (baritone horn), and two sisters, Pearl and Beryl Wire (both tenor horns). They stand facing the old fire station, now the current Salvation Army hall, with their backs to the canal. Mary Jones and her cousin Ena used to practise in the shed at the bottom of the garden and Mary, now 77, remembers Uncle Dick (Griggs), patience exhausted, striding down the garden to tell them to be quiet. Her grandmother and great uncle were members of the Cloake family, who were responsible for Hythe's successful fishing fleet, and they were closely involved with the Griggs family who, their fishing interests apart, were largely responsible for the development of the Salvation Army Corps in Hythe, which celebrated its centenary in 1996. There are still memories of the early meetings in the 'Tar Pot' in Albert Lane.

The Salvation Army boys' band in 1935. The boys' band played at Sunday School in the mornings and with the senior band on Sunday afternoons—in winter in the senior hall and in summer on the seafront. Although the boys' band is not active today, youngsters of both sexes are being trained and take part in many Salvation Army activities. From left to right, back row: Ted Mills, John Mills, Ronald But, Ronald Murgatroyd, Pat Watts, Sonny Griggs, ? Thompson, George Becket, ? Murgatroyd (brother of Ronald). Second Row: Douglas Akehurst, Mr Bennet (drummer), Phil Akehurst (band leader), Major Thompson, Wright Griggs, Colin But. Front row: Harold Bennet, Mark Godden, Eric Blackman, Kenneth Woods.

The town band. There is a strong musical tradition in Hythe. Today, bands still play in front of the town hall and, on some summer Sunday afternoons, on the bandstand, when many residents enjoy this 'old-fashioned' pleasure.

A parade to commemorate the end of the First World War takes place in Hythe's High Street, with thankful townspeople walking alongside. Cave's Café can be seen on the left side, and Lee's Toy Shop features on the right. Behind the band march ex-servicemen wearing their medals.

The Hythe Military Band, pictured here in 1898. Top row: J. E. Elgar, W. Cooper, C. Durez, W. Mayne, W. Friend, T. G. Perkins, C. Webb. Second row: H. Harris, H. Beach, C. J. Eeles, A. Miller, H. Horton, F. Arnold, E. Gosbee, C. Wood, T. G. Bates. Bottom row: R. E. Potter, D. Arnold, A. J. Horton, H. J. Godden, J. H. C. Nelson (bandmaster), W. Austin, H. Stapleton, J. T. Edwards, H. Alger. Four men were absent.

The bandstand once stood in the Grove, which was the area between Ladies' Bridge and the Town Bridge, alongside the canal. Today it is in the nearby grounds of Oaklands. Above, a concert is in progress, enjoyed by a seated audience and passers-by. Any band playing today on the bandstand immediately attracts an audience.

Fourteen

Journey's End

On a bright summer's day, a ride in the tram that followed the coastline from Sandgate to Hythe could be very pleasant. In the early days, trams were pulled by horses, but after the First World War many of the mules returning from France ended their days pulling trams.

The corner of Stade Street and South Road before the First World War. Donkeys are being taken to the beach, with an accompaniment of children, while adults sit back comfortably in a horse-drawn tram, which is just turning into South Road.

People dismounting in front of the Red Lion Hotel, in Red Lion Square at the top of the High Street, during the 1890s. The High Street, a well-known shopping centre, was a favourite destination. Coach and horses were still the main form of transport, but Red Lion Square was also the terminus for the tram (centre).

Public transport waiting at the tram terminus with steps leading to the upper deck. Although the horse-drawn tram is still running, it is now joined by a motor vehicle (left), around which a group of people are standing. It was evidently an attraction: the message on the postcard reads, 'How should you like to be motoring over to Folkestone?'

The scene in Red Lion Square (also known as Market Square) in 1890. Apart from this one lady with an umbrella, rain has deterred other shoppers, and the horse-drawn tram remains empty. An early member of the Spicer family (see 'The Old Curiosity Shop') remembered that 'the backs of the seats would be pushed forward or back at the end of the journey so that everyone sat facing the front. On rough days they were positioned to afford some comfort.' The vehicle was affectionately nicknamed 'the toast-rack'.

Left: This Victorian photograph shows a heavily-laden cart leaving the old water mill, at the end of the High Street, possibly carrying a load of flour. The waterwheel of the mill has since been renovated and the building refurbished and converted into a comfortable house belonging to the Marston family, who have long been active in local business circles and still help to run the Marston Hotel Group, which owns the Imperial Hotel in Hythe.

Below: Shoeing in progress at the Old Forge in Chapel Street—still there, though not always open. A number of different horses came to be shod, like carthorses and those drawing the baker's, grocer's and butcher's vans that were familiar sights on the streets of many English towns up to the 1950s.

The Metropole Laundry in Hythe, with its unmistakable chimney, in the early 1900s. A horse-drawn van outside the building in Sandgate Road was still used for deliveries and collection.

Gradually, journeys of all descriptions began to be taken by motorized vehicles. Here a young driver for the Metropole Laundry in Hythe obviously relishes his three-wheel van.

Despite all the various forms of transport on offer, Shanks's Pony remains popular, particularly in Hythe's famous Ladies' Walk. Here, walkers enjoy watching a game of tennis while others take a leisurely afternoon stroll. Elizabeth Bowen wrote in her novel, *The House in Paris*: 'Across

fields dry with salt air, the straight shady Ladies' Walk, with lamps strung from the branches, runs down from the town to the sea: on hot days a cool way to walk and bathe.'

Left: Mr and Mrs Wood and their three children, Tom, Frank and Margaret, in their horse-drawn carriage, go visiting in their Sunday best. This was the preferred form of transport around the Hythe countryside in the early twentieth century. Today, fast cars vie with each other on these same country roads, yet just off these roads, a surprising amount of quiet and peacefulness still remains.

Below: Virtually no traffic was on the country roads when Fred Clark, the driver of this car, took his passengers out for a spin. The car will raise many a nostalgic sigh, with its hood, running board and large spare wheel (which might be stolen within minutes today).

Laurel and Hardy drew the crowds when they went for a ride on the tiny R. H. D. [Romney, Hythe and Dymchurch] light railway, a five gauge railway, which travels across the marshes and is still a major attraction to children today, especially on 'Thomas the Tank-Engine' days, and at Christmas when they run 'Santa Specials'.

An adult-sized train at Hythe Station: the service and the station are no longer there after having being axed by Dr Beeching. This is a great loss to the travelling public as it was possible to reach any destination in the country on the railway, even if it did involve time-consuming branch-line travel.

Members of the Hythe Cyclists' Touring Club c.1880. From left to right: Mr Simpson, Mr A. Capon, Mr H. Godden and Mr F. Worthington. In those days cycling was considered to be highly dangerous, so much so that cyclists often telegraphed their families to say they had reached their destination safely. Not everyone liked the sport—many irate people wrote to newspapers to say that cyclists should be banned from the roads. Photograph courtesy of The Old Gallery Bookshop, Hythe.